HOW TO BE A GREAT BOSS :ways to unleash your potential to become an inspirational and successful boss are in this book"HOW TO BE A GREAT BOSS"

William R. Cline

Table of content

Chapter 1

Chapter 2

Chapter 3

Chapter 4

Chapter 5

Chapter 6

Chapter 1

How to surround yourself with great people.

Positive individuals will encourage and support you, and they will be there to lend a hand when you need it. Surround yourself with such people. When attempting to accomplish your goals—which can be challenging to perform on your own—this can be of great assistance. You have a higher chance of success if you have the help of others.

Never forget that your ultimate identity is shaped by the people you spend the most time with. You need to surround yourself with individuals who push you as well as inspire you if you want to achieve new heights of achievement. Although it's not always simple, it's worthwhile.

content workers at the office

1. MAKE THE CHOICE TO ESCAPE FROM GREATNESS

Everybody has goals in life, but which ones are essential in your book? Your relationships and the activities you choose to devote your time to are reflections of your standards. Are you attempting to expand your company? If so, why would you choose to surround yourself with negative and distracting people? Committing to improving your standards right now is the best way to start surrounding yourself with positive energy.

Perhaps you're concerned about moving on or you've just grown accustomed to having particular folks around. Keep fear from ruining your life. The bar for what you will and won't accept in your life and business is raised when you consciously decide to surround yourself with positive individuals who share your goals and bring you joy. You will be unstoppable once you realize that your dreams and goals are worthwhile.

2. DISCARD UNFAVORABLE RELATIONSHIPS

Do your team and business partners lack ambition, even though you consider yourself a go-getter? Are those close to you preventing you from reaching the next level of achievement that you're striving for? Making changes with your peers or coworkers starts with figuring out who in your life is dragging you down. You will have more time to surround yourself with successful people if you let go of bad relationships.

The easiest method to identify these people is to consider your feelings following your interactions with them. Are you confident in yourself and up for new challenges? Or do you feel angry, self-conscious, and unable to regulate your feelings? Our emotions are a gift that informs us of things we need to modify to feel more content. They are there to tell us things. Someone isn't beneficial for you if, after spending time with them, you feel exhausted, afraid, or agitated.

Releasing yourself from unsatisfactory relationships is often uncomfortable. Since you may have known some of these friends or coworkers for a long time, you don't want to sour relations. However, it's crucial to avoid feeling beholden to them or thinking that you owe them anything just because they are "old friends." To transform your perspective and set yourself free, ascertain what motivates you to continue in these relationships. You'll be more equipped to concentrate on the things that are most important to you and your company.

3. Recognize positive individuals
Be in the company of positive and kind individuals.

You presumably already have some supportive individuals in your life, even though you also undoubtedly have some bad relationships. They don't have to be the same; in fact, having a variety of personality types in your organization will be advantageous. When you need to surround yourself with positive individuals, it's good to have these four categories of people in your inner circle.

knowledgeable individuals. Being surrounded by intelligent people will encourage you to never stop learning and to maintain your curiosity, two qualities that are crucial for people who go on to excel in business.

diligent workers. Success is more than just intelligence; in fact, many intelligent people lack the motivation to succeed. A diligent worker's hunger motivates those around them to strive for greater things in life.

Visionaries and dreamers. Dreamers are just as important to the world as doers are. The person in your group with the most vision is the one who will listen to your wildest ideas and never stop motivating you to follow your dreams.

optimistic minds. While not everyone is content all the time, some people view challenges as chances, while others view them as insurmountable barriers. You want the first kind of person in your life when times are hard.

4. APPLY TO FORM A PROFESSIONAL GROUP

Ascending the success ladder faster is possible if you surround yourself with knowledgeable people. Discovering a mentor is a great method to be surrounded by successful individuals. Tony will tell you that nobody succeeds on their own and that he was mentored numerous times in his life. Someone who is already achieving the outcomes you desire can serve as a mentor. Whether they realize it or not, they have a successful strategy, and by spending time with them, you may create a strategy of your own. What is this person's dispute resolution process? How do they connect with important people and build relationships? What routines have they developed that have contributed to their success? Examine their habits and consider how you can incorporate comparable ones into your own life.

You can also work with a business coach who can assist you in overcoming limiting beliefs and finding positive individuals to spend time with, or you can join an online or offline mastermind group or other professional organization. The coach will not only be a nice companion, but they will also be able to assist you in determining which people in your life you should spend less time with and in finding new opportunities to build positive relationships.

5. LEAVE YOUR ZONE OF COMFORT

"Every growth begins at the edge of your comfort zone," as Tony once said. You must spend time with the kind of individuals who will elevate you if you want to surround yourself with them. Aspiring individuals participate in intellectually stimulating lectures and workshops that push them beyond their comfort zones. They continuously push themselves outside their comfort zones and expose themselves to others who have diverse viewpoints.

Tony Robbins has worked with influential people and top business executives in a variety of industries for decades. Tony has acquired the skills required for any firm to succeed by surrounding himself with the greatest in the industry. World-class presenters and like-minded people who are eager to achieve will be around you at Business Mastery, the five-day event that will completely change your company.

Hear from professionals and network with like-minded individuals who are looking for information to grow their businesses. Attending Business Mastery and achieving success in your life show you that your aspirations are worthwhile, and you meet some of the world's most motivated and industrious people.

Chapter 2

How to make more effective use of your time.

The practice of deciding how much time to spend on various tasks is known as time management. Effective time management reduces stress, makes it possible to accomplish more in less time, and promotes job success.

picture of hands holding time management and associated themes paper cards

Time management advantages
It's critical to have good time management skills. Effective time management promotes increased productivity and efficiency, reduced stress, and more success in life. The following are some advantages of efficient time management:

1. Relieving stress

Anxiety is decreased when a task schedule is created and followed. You may see that you are moving closer to your goals as you cross tasks off your "to-do" list. By doing this, you can prevent yourself from being anxious about whether you're doing tasks.

2. Extra time
You can spend more time in your daily life when you practice good time management. Effective time managers like having extra time for their hobbies and other personal interests.

3. More chances
Effective time management creates more opportunities and reduces time lost on pointless activities. One of the main things that companies look for is good time management abilities. For every business, being able to schedule and prioritize tasks is quite important.

4. Capacity to achieve objectives

People who have effective time management skills can accomplish goals and objectives more quickly and with greater effectiveness.

A Compendium of Time Management Hints
After reviewing the advantages of time management, let's examine some efficient time management techniques:

An infographic with time management advice

1. Establish realistic goals
Establish quantifiable and attainable goals. When creating goals, follow the SMART approach. To put it simply, make sure the objectives you set are Timely, Relevant, Specific, Measurable, and Attainable.

2. Set sensible priorities
Sort tasks according to their urgency and importance. Consider your everyday responsibilities, for instance, and identify which are:

Important and urgent: Take immediate action on these things.

Appropriate but not urgent: Choose a time to complete these chores.

Important but urgent: If at all possible, assign these chores to others.

Put things off till later; they are neither urgent nor crucial.

3. Assign a deadline for finishing a task.

Establishing deadlines for work makes you more productive and focused. It can also assist you in identifying possible issues before they arise if you take a little extra time to determine how much time you need to allocate for each task. In this manner, you can prepare strategies for handling them.

Let's say, for instance, that you have five reviews to write up before a meeting. But you know that with the time left before the meeting, you can only finish four of them. You might be able to assign writing one of the reviews to someone else if you are aware of this fact well in advance. On the other hand, you might not have realized your time issue until an hour before the meeting if you hadn't bothered to run a time check on your responsibilities beforehand. By then, it could be much harder to locate someone to assign one of the reviews to, and it might also be harder for them to fit the assignment into their schedule.

4. Take a rest in between jobs.
Performing a large number of chores nonstop makes it more difficult to remain motivated and concentrated. Take a little break in between jobs to refuel and clear your mind. Think about taking a quick nap, taking a quick stroll, or practicing meditation.

5. Get yourself in order.
Make better long-term use of your calendar to manage your time. Note down the due dates for assignments or projects that need to be completed to finish the larger work.

Consider the days that would work best for completing particular chores. For instance, you might need to schedule a meeting to talk about cash flow for a day when you know the CFO of the company will be free.

6. Eliminate any unnecessary chores or activities

Eliminating unnecessary duties or activities is crucial. Assess what is important and worthy of your time. You may spend more of your time on things that are important when you eliminate duties and activities that aren't necessary.

7. Make a plan in advance

Make sure you know exactly what has to be done each day when you wake up each morning. Think about developing the habit of writing out your "to-do" list for the following weekday as soon as each workday ends. In this manner, the next morning, you can get started right away.

Consequences of Ineffective Time Management

Let's also talk about the negative effects of ineffective time management.

1. Ineffective workflow

Poor efficiency is the result of not being able to set goals and make advance plans. An efficient strategy would be to finish related jobs concurrently or sequentially, for instance, if multiple crucial chores need to be finished. But if you don't make a strategy, you can find yourself needing to go back and forth, or backtrack, while working. This results in decreased production and efficiency.

2. Time lost

Time is lost as a result of poor time management. For instance, you are wasting time and distracting yourself when you use social media to converse with pals while working on an assignment.

3. A loss of command

You experience a lack of control over your life when you are unsure of what has to be done next. That may be a factor in increased worry and stress.

4. Subpar output

Your job will usually suffer in quality if you have poor time management skills. For instance, rushing to finish assignments at the last minute typically results in a compromise in quality.

5. A bad image

Clients' and your employer's expectations and opinions of you suffer if they can't count on you to finish assignments on time. A client will probably go elsewhere if they can't count on you to complete an assignment on time.

Chapter 3

How to create accountability.

It's impossible to create a high-performing team when there's a lack of accountability.

Accountability is when people take responsibility for their own actions. It's about taking initiative and recognizing not only that individuals have the power to cause problems, but also to fix them. In this article, we'll dive into what accountability looks like at work, why it's essential and how to embed it into your culture:

What does accountability mean in the workplace?

What happens when there's a lack of accountability at work?

How do you show accountability at work?

7 steps to make accountability a core part of your culture.

6 more steps to build accountability in your organization.

Ways for holding coworkers accountable.

What does accountability mean in the workplace?

Accountability in the workplace means that all employees are responsible for their actions, behaviors, performance and decisions. It's also linked to an increase in commitment to work and employee morale, which leads to higher performance.

It's recognizing that other team members and general company performance depend on the results of your work. When employees are held accountable, they take responsibility for results and don't assume it's someone else's job.

Essentially, it's the opposite of passing the buck.

The directly responsible individual
The concept of the directly responsible individual (DRI), coined by Apple, is the perfect example of accountability at work. Everything at Apple, big or small, is assigned to someone who's directly responsible for it.

DRIs are held accountable for the success and failure of the projects they're assigned to. By explicitly assigning responsibility, there's less room for passing blame, and more clarity over who's making decisions.

Ultimately, when team members consistently demonstrate ownership and accountability, trust is formed. This results in less micromanaging and higher performance.

What happens when there's a lack of accountability at work?
To put it simply: A lack of accountability damages the team.

When people aren't accountable, one person's delay becomes the team's delay. One shortfall snowballs into bigger shortfalls.

When missed deadlines, lack of punctuality, and unfinished work are tolerated, they have the tendency to become the norm. People learn that the real deadline is a week from the published one; that consistently being 10 minutes late for a meeting is okay; that sub-par work is acceptable. Your team suffers, and ultimately your workplace culture suffers too.

Lack of accountability
Having a member of the team that isn't meeting their commitments and isn't being held accountable causes frustration and disengagement with the rest of the team.

According to Partners In Leadership, a lack of accountability in the workplace leads to:

Low team morale.

Unclear priorities across the team.

Decreased employee engagement.

Unmet team and individual goals.

Low levels of trust.

High turnover.

How do you show accountability at work?
Clearly, there's a high cost for a lack of accountability. So how do you either avoid

or remedy the situation? Before even thinking about how to embed accountability into your workplace culture, you need to look within. Are you demonstrating accountability at work?

Goals and expectations are a good place to start. You can't be accountable if you don't know what you should be taking accountability for. Set goals for yourself and your team that are clear and measurable so everyone, including you, knows what you're trying to achieve.

Next, you'll want to address the gap between expectations and performance. Once you understand your goals and expectations, you can bridge the gap between what you're actually doing and what you're supposed to be doing. Is there an abyss where things are getting lost because you didn't realize they fell on your plate?

Lastly, and most importantly, take responsibility for your actions. When you acknowledge you've made a mistake, you're also recognizing you have the power to fix that mistake. And that's the beauty of accountability.

Examples of demonstrating your own accountability in the workplace:
Complete tasks that have been assigned to you by the timeline you agreed on.
Be responsible for the success of your team and make the effort to support your team when needed.
When you schedule meetings, respect everyone else's time by showing up prepared and on time (and expect that others do too).
Take ownership over the problems you flag by coming to the table with solutions too.
Don't sweep problems under the rug or assume the issue's already being dealt with. Instead, flag issues as they arise.
How to make accountability a core part of your culture and a core value of your team

We resist holding others accountable because we're uncomfortable doing it, we forget to do it or maybe we don't even know how to go about it. Here's how to tackle these issues to create a culture of accountability in the workplace.

1. Lead by example and hold yourself accountable first

Like we mentioned earlier, as a manager, you're the pacesetter of tone, performance, and culture for your team. People will follow your lead. If you're continuously showing up to meetings late, pushing deadlines, and not owning up to your mistakes, the team will follow suit.

Pacesetting definition

2. Set team goals

Setting goals is an essential part of creating a culture of accountability on your team. It helps establish what you're trying to achieve together.

But it's important to remember not all goals are made equal. To set goals that encourage accountability, they need to be measurable, clear and challenging. Our favorite way to set goals is through the OKR framework (objective and key results). The beauty of OKRs is that they're not top-down. You create them together as a team and they're easily trackable. Plus, they should ladder up to larger company goals so everyone know their impact on the bigger picture.

This makes it easier for everyone to understand their roles and what's expected on both an individual and team level.

3. Work on your feedback skills
Giving tough feedback isn't easy, but it's a skill that can be improved. One of the most important things you do as a manager is to provide feedback. When you regularly give feedback (including positive feedback), it makes tough feedback much easier to give.

It also reduces the chance of your direct report being surprised by the feedback they're receiving, leading to further disengagement.

There are a few ingredients that make up effective feedback:

Ensure psychological safety: It's essential to give negative feedback in a safe, private space, like your one-on-one meetings. But it's important to remember psychological safety doesn't happen over night. Work to create a space with your team members where they feel comfortable being vulnerable and being themselves. If they don't, it's going to be a lot harder for them to accept your feedback.

Assume positive intent: At its heart, effective feedback comes from a place of genuinely wanting to help someone grow. You need to 'give a damn.' And vice-versa, assume the issue you're addressing wasn't done with mal intent. It comes down to having eachother's backs.

Be specific: When you're too general, you're not doing your team member any favors. Use a specific example to back up your feedback — that way they'll have a better understanding of how to improve.

4. Create a culture of two-way feedback

Good feedback isn't only about the ability to give it, it's also about being open to receiving it and providing a space to do so. When you don't foster a culture of two-way feedback, and your team members don't feel like there's a safe space to speak up, they start to disengage. Vital Smarts studied nearly 800 professionals and found that:

52% hesitate to discuss peer performance problems, like improper shortcuts, poor attention to detail and incomplete work
47% say they wait to share concerns or ideas that might improve an element of the

business because it encroaches on somebody else's turf

49% take more than a week to speak up when policy decisions are begining to create unintended negative consequences

55% are reluctant to discuss when they believe someone (or a group) has made a bad strategic choice

That's a lot of valuable insights that are being missed, and resources being wasted. It's important to encourage two-way feedback so your team feels confident identifying and communicating problems.

5.Make accountability a habit

Setting up a reminder to give and solicit feedback as part of each meeting agenda will help ensure that feedback flows consistently. We believe one-on-ones and team meetings are great opportunities to build a habit around accountability.

Here are a few of the meeting questions that managers using Hypercontext add to their one-on-one agendas to make accountability a habit:

-Is there anything we should START doing as a team?
-Would you like more or less direction from me on your work?
-Do you feel you're getting enough feedback on your work? If not, where would you like more feedback?
-Is there an aspect of your job where you would like more help or coaching?
-How could we improve the ways our team works together?

6. Keep track of your commitments and hold each other accountable
If you make a promise to provide more feedback to your direct reports, make sure you add that as a future agenda item to hold yourself accountable. If your employee commits to providing a work back schedule for a project by a certain date, make sure you have a way to check-in on that day.

One easy way to foster a culture of accountability – or, if the damage has already been done, address a lack of accountability – is to make sure you're assigning action items during meetings.

This is a perfect way to hold each and every member of your team accountable for their actions. In Hypercontext, for example, our Next Steps feature allows you to assign action items to team members, complete with deadlines, right in each meeting agenda item. You can't close the agenda item until all the next steps are complete, so the team has a clear picture of what's being done – and who needs to be held accountable for tasks that have been missed.

7. Use an accountability framework
A lack of accountability is rarely intentional. Often, it's a result of other problems — one being unclear roles and responsibilities.

When there's a lack of clarity around who's responsible for what, it makes accountability nearly impossible. In fact, a Gallup study found that only 50% of employees strongly indicate that they know what's expected of them at work.

Luckily, accountability frameworks like the RACI matrix can help with this problem. Also known as a RACI chart, this accountability framework ensures everyone involved with a project is assigned a role every step of the way. These roles are broken out into 4 levels of accountability:

Responsible: Those who are responsible for completing the task at hand.
Accountable: Those who are ultimately accountable for the completion of the task or deliverable. This individual is also responsible for delegating the work to those who are responsible for completing it.
Consulted: These individuals are typically the subject-matter experts on the task at

hand. They are involved in the specific stage of the project in a consulting and advisory capacity.

Informed: These are the individuals who are kept up-to-date on progress at each stage of the project. This is usually done in the form of one-way communication.

6 more steps to build accountability in your organization.

People want to be surrounded by reliable coworkers who follow through well, deliver on what's required, and do it on time. Work would be much simpler if everyone was reliable more often. Much of this falls on an organization's culture around accountability.

Exhibit the Standard
Building a culture of accountability starts with you, the leader of the team. Your goal of fostering a culture of accountability has

no chance if you're not able to lead the way by exhibiting the standard.

If you, the leader of your organization, are not accountable for your actions, outcomes, and work, it's going to be very, very hard to build a culture of accountability among those around you.

Others will follow your lead. What you choose to do, or not do, will set the standard for what is acceptable and not acceptable.

If you can't exhibit the standard, building a culture of accountability will be near impossible.

Clarify and Document Expectations
When leading a team, focus on clarifying and documenting the most important outcomes of what needs to be accomplished. What are the metrics, results, and outcomes that really matter?

Clarify expectations. Document them. Assign ownership to accomplishing them. Make it clear.

Clear expectations must have three things:

A clear owner: who is responsible for delivery?
A clear result: upon completion, it should be easy to answer the question, "was the expected outcome achieved or not?"
A clear timeline: upon completion, it should be easy to answer the question, "was the result achieved on time?
These expectations can be as large or granular as needed. The key is creating clarity.

When clarified, make sure the expectations are written down somewhere so that those assigning them and those who are responsible for them have visibility.

Gain Acknowledgement (and Hopefully, Agreement)

It's important to make sure that those who are assigned expectations understand and acknowledge what needs to be accomplished and by when it needs to be accomplished. Again, get really clear here.

Work to clarify any unknowns together. Ensure that those who are responsible acknowledge what's expected of them.

Provide Resources, Training, and Support

Reasonable resources, training, and support should be provided for anyone working to meet the expectations assigned to them.

They should have everything they need around them to be successful. If they don't have the resources, training, or support, it's likely they won't meet what's expected. As a leader, part of your responsibility is to set your team members up for success. Aligning resources, training, and support with what needs to be accomplished is vital.

Coach to Correct
If and when expectations are not met, a leader's job is to coach until the expectations are met.

That might mean more training. That might mean allocating more resources. That might mean a hard conversation about what someone is and isn't capable of.

When expectations aren't met, is must be addressed.

Otherwise, your culture of accountability falters.

Reward Follow Through
When expectations are met, celebrate it!

Make following through and being accountable a positive part of your organization's culture. Show that following through and driving the right outcomes is what matters. Do it often enough and it will become contagious.

Culture is Built Through Established Norms
Your established norms mold your team's culture.

If a lack of accountability and poor follow-through is not met with correction in your organization, that behavior becomes acceptable.

But by driving with a focus on follow-through and making that an everyday expectation, leaders can build a strong culture of accountability that helps their organization thrive in the present and future.

Ways for holding coworkers accountable.

Creating a culture of accountability on your direct team is one story. Holding your peers accountable is another one. How do you hold your coworkers accountable so you can optimize the way you work together across the whole organization?

Contrary to popular belief, holding your coworkers accountable isn't about pointing fingers or assigning blame. It boils down to supporting one another. Here are some key things to consider to create more accountability with your coworkers:

Be transparent: Be open and honest with your colleagues. Sometimes, we hold our cards close due to tricky work politics, or working in silos. But, being open helps create accountability, both for yourself and your peers.

Support each other: Working in silos is a quick way to foster a lack of accountability for anything that happens beyond your team. But, the reality is that an organization is a puzzle and each team is a piece of the whole picture. You need to work together to achieve your company goals. Even if it might be 'outside of your job description,' see where you can support each other. Their problems are your problems too.

Don't forget about peer-to-peer one-on-ones: One-on-ones are too often reserved for manager/direct report relationships. But peer-to-peer one-on-ones are an important part of building empathy and accountability through the organization. It's easy to put the blame for a project gone wrong onto another team. But, if you're connecting with your peers with recurring meetings, you can better understand blockers and limitations and have greater context to decisions being made on their team.

Chapter 4

How to develop productive, relationships with each of your people.

Those who have a best buddy at work are seven times more likely to be involved in their work, per the Gallup organization. However, it is not required to be a "BFF." According to research from Gallup, having a close friend at work increases happiness. [1] Furthermore, improved customer engagement and higher profit are associated with positive work relationships.

This article will teach you the value of having positive professional connections, as well as how to create and preserve them and even find methods to collaborate with people you don't get along with.

Why Build Strong Professional Bonds?
People are sociable creatures by nature. Furthermore, having positive working

connections with our coworkers will make our jobs more fun given that we spend one-third of our lives at work.[2]

Coworkers will feel more confident to voice thoughts, discuss, and accept new ideas, for example, if they are more at ease with one another. It takes this kind of cooperation to embrace change, develop, and invent. And group morale and productivity surge when members witness the successes of working together in this way.

You can be free in relationships at work as well. You can concentrate on opportunities instead of wasting time and energy on unfavorable connections, such as gaining new business or concentrating on your growth.

Additionally, maintaining a strong professional network will help you advance in your career by providing access to chances that you might not otherwise have.

What Makes a Relationship Good?

Trust, respect, self-awareness, inclusivity, and open communication are necessary for a healthy working partnership. Let's examine each of these traits individually.

Trust: You can be forthright and honest in your thoughts and deeds when you have faith in your teammates. Furthermore, you can stop wasting time and effort "watching your back."

Mutual respect among team members allows them to value each other's opinions and come up with solutions based on their combined knowledge, experience, and inventiveness.

Self-awareness entails accepting accountability for your deeds and words as well as resisting the urge to let your bad feelings affect those around you.

Include everyone: extend a warm welcome to those with different backgrounds and viewpoints! When your coworkers have different ideas than you, for example, consider their viewpoints and insights—a "cultural add"—while making decisions.

Honest and transparent communication is the foundation of all successful partnerships. The better you communicate with those around you, whether through video calls or emails, in-person meetings, or both, the more connected you will be.

Which Professional Relationships Are Crucial?

While it's important to establish and preserve positive working relationships with everyone, certain individuals require particular consideration. similar to that of an employer and employee. According to research by Gallup, a manager alone can explain as much as 70% of a team's engagement. [3]

Managers and staff can develop relationships through regular one-on-one meetings. During these follow-ups, you can help someone understand how their work fits into the organization's "bigger picture," highlight their strengths and help them identify areas that need improvement.

To better understand your manager's working style, anticipate their demands, and modify your approach for a more harmonious working relationship, you might also investigate managing upwards.

Building strong working ties with important stakeholders will also help you. These are the people, like your team, suppliers, and customers, who stand to gain or lose from your business. Developing a relationship with them can assist you in keeping your career and projects on schedule. To dedicate effort to forming these alliances, a stakeholder analysis aids in identifying these individuals.

Advice: Establishing personal ties might result from tight collaboration with others. If that occurs to you, our article on How to

Handle a Personal Relationship at Work can help you handle the situation professionally and protect both your relationship and your company's reputation during working hours.

How to Create Strong Professional Bonds

Your oldest friends will attest to the fact that developing deep relationships with people can take time and work. However, there are also a few easy things you can do to improve the rapport you have with your coworkers.

Determine Your Needs in a Relationship. Do you know what other people can do for you? And what is it that they require from you? Improving relationships can be facilitated by having a greater understanding of these demands.

Boost Your Interpersonal Skills. Good people skills are the foundation of good partnerships. Try our quiz. How Effective Are You with People? to evaluate your teamwork, communication, and conflict resolution skills. The assessment will also direct you to helpful resources to strengthen any areas of weakness.

Pay Attention to Your EI. The capacity to identify and interpret your own emotions more effectively is known as emotional intelligence (EI). You'll get better at recognizing and responding to other people's needs and emotions as your emotional intelligence (EI) grows.

Engage in Mindful Listening. Individuals who genuinely listen to others tend to get along better with them. You'll comprehend more and talk less if you listen mindfully. And people will rapidly come to trust you.

Make Time for Developing Connections. Try inviting a coworker out for a quick cup of coffee if at all possible. Alternatively, perform a "one-minute kindness" by leaving a note on a colleague's LinkedIn post that you found interesting or by sending them a brief message to see how they're doing. Although they take time, these insignificant exchanges set the foundation for enduring bonds.

Control Your Limitations. Allow enough time, but not too much! Relationships at work can occasionally hinder productivity, particularly if a buddy or coworker starts taking up all of your time. It's critical to establish limits and control the amount of time you spend interacting with coworkers.

Respect Others. Everyone wants to feel as though their effort is valued, both their supervisor and the intern. Thus, when someone in your immediate vicinity does anything well, sincerely thank them. Strong professional relationships can be facilitated by praise and acknowledgment.

Think positively. Concentrate on being upbeat. individuals are drawn to happy individuals because positivity is contagious.

Steer clear of gossip. Workplace relationships can be ruined by gossip and office politics. Address the issue directly with the member of your group with whom you are at odds. Spreading rumors among coworkers will only make matters worse by increasing distrust and hostility.

Managing Tough Workplace Relationships
You may have to collaborate with someone you don't get along with sometimes. A break from one another is helping many coworkers, especially with the rise of virtual offices. However, miscommunication or conflict can arise even when conversing digitally.

Avoiding conflict-causing individuals is natural, but it's not always possible and might weaken team dynamics. Here are some strategies for preserving or repairing a business connection.

Think back to your successful past. Research indicates that remembering pleasant times spent with a coworker might mend a strained connection if things have gone wrong following an incident. Utilizing an unbiased mediator to help heal divisions and find a speedy settlement is an additional choice.

Consider yourself. When we have bad feelings for someone, we can lose our patience, get upset, and discourage other people. And we might expect the same negative behaviors in return from others. The Betari Box can assist in interrupting this destructive pattern of behavior and attitudes, putting an end to them.

Set goals that will benefit both parties. Have you ever thought that a power imbalance could be the cause of a challenging relationship? To find any competing objectives or power disparities, apply Professor John Eldred's power tactics model. Then, come up with a plan to strengthen your relationship and increase communication.

Chapter 5

How to deal with direct reports that don't meet your expectations.

This is not acceptable at all. It implies that rather than being a productive member of a team, he or she is purposefully undermining what I am attempting to do. The cohesiveness of the team as a whole deteriorates the longer this is allowed. I would:

Collect and review the evidence
Try to uncover less harmful reasons, if any can be found, and suggest potential other theories.
Determine whether or if this may be salvaged by confronting: Sometimes, with the appropriate approach, drive may be instilled, and if it's feasible, I'd like to turn someone into an ally.
If the situation cannot be saved, talk about the next steps, such as giving other team

members more responsibility and allowing the person to submit a resignation.
Achievement

It is possible to manage subpar performance. Managing a low performance needs planning and consistent, continuous work. On the other hand, since your team is the basis for your manager evaluation, it's a significant time investment. As a result, I would

1. Compile & review the evidence

2. Look for less harmful explanations and try to explore potential alternates, such as miscommunication or misunderstanding, training, private issues, work style, etc. If it can be fixed, create a plan to do so.

3. Have a meeting with the employee to talk about subpar work and get an explanation. Talk about the various hypotheses and come up with a strategy that includes as much of

the important information from step 2 as is practical. Explain the timeframe and the consequences of not improving.

4.Keep an eye on things, check in once a week or more frequently as needed, and wish for success. If the deadline is missed, talk to a staff member and start the separation procedure. Plus plus. A very senior man who had recently been promoted to vice president and now reported to me instead of the CEO or me sought a significant shareholder on the board of directors to elevate him to the position and establish his training division as a stand-alone department, independent of HR. The CEO was incensed when the shareholder informed him, and he asked me what I intended to do about it. Even if we asked him if he could work correctly without engaging in any further insubordination—it's a yes-or-no question—we all knew the person would be disruptive, dissatisfied, and insubordinate.

He saw it as obviously no. Even though it wasn't what he wanted, I managed to get him out of the company in a way that suited everyone. The main takeaway is that insubordination must end right away and must not make the employee feel bad about their employment, or they must resign. The scenario will determine how you proceed. Sometimes someone will say that they won't be insubordinate, but they won't follow through on that promise. In that case, you'll need to follow the necessary steps to fire them as quickly as possible.

It's critical to make a sincere effort to support an employee who is performing poorly. It takes longer to complete. You take them down and, in a calm and considerate manner, go over what they do well (importantly) and what needs improvement. Then, if they are positive and understanding, you may assist them find another position inside or outside the company, or you can support them in a learning program if they want to stay. Together, you decide how they will learn or leave when the time comes (it's their choice). You revisit them after a fair amount of time has passed to assess development and repeat the procedure. You may have to decide on termination processes without their input at some time, since it typically becomes evident to both of you whether or not things have improved sufficiently. For example, is severance pay due (which it is not in most "employment at will" states in the US, but it is in most other countries), etc.

Chapter 6

The five leadership practices and five management practices of all great bosses.

The abundance of models explaining what leaders actually do may worry you if you believe there are several definitions of leadership.

But there is a workable strategy that has proven successful in a variety of government agencies and nonprofit organizations that we have collaborated with. The paradigm, called Leadership Practices, was created by researchers Kouzes and Posner based on Tom Peters' original research.

Over the course of the first five years, Kouzes and Posner conducted research with over 1,000 high-achieving leaders to see what made them successful. It was also crucial to include their "followers" in this study.

Combining the two viewpoints, the study effort comprised questioning followers and leaders about:

What attributes When leaders were at their most successful, they felt they needed
What attributes persons in leadership felt were crucial when they perceived themselves as effective leaders
After the data was analyzed, the research team saw a pattern of agreement between leaders and those being led regarding the actions that motivated people to achieve remarkable feats within organizations. Afterwards, these were formalized as the five leadership practices. Depending on the difficulties you encounter, the particular practices required and their attributes may change, but eventually you will need to use them all.

According to leaders and followers, when they are performing at their peak, leaders challenge, inspire, enable, model, and encourage. And they achieved this by making a commitment to specific behaviors and moral principles. Kouzes and Posner have conclusively demonstrated that these behaviors were an observable and learnable collection of practices in the twenty years since the model was initially developed. They created training to guarantee that anyone willing to put in the necessary time to master the techniques could do so. Based on this training, =mc has developed a model that we currently heavily utilize for both internal and external projects.

Additionally, Kouzes and Posner created a 360° Inventory to assist in determining each person's:

current degree of proficiency in each activity, as judged by them and others, where they still have room to grow in order to empower their team and meet organizational goals

Take note that Kouzes and Posner refer to these attributes as practices, meaning that people must genuinely engage in these activities for them to be evident.

The Five Leadership Practices.
The five practices and their implications for leaders are explained in more depth here.

1. Question the procedure
According to Kouzes and Posner's research, leaders grow and learn from adversity and challenging circumstances. They are risk-takers who view failure as an opportunity to grow and develop, provided it is not the result of subpar work. They are early adopters as well. They look for solutions that seem to work and then demand that they be enhanced. They provide challenges all the time.

This technique implies that "business as usual" is not something we should be satisfied with. In order to lead, you must:

Seek out difficult chances to develop, adapt, create, and advance both personally and organizationally.

Try new things, take chances, and inspire others to do the same. Establish a culture where individuals believe they can grow from the errors that come with it.

Think about the aspects of your organization's work that require questioning, including the ones that appear to be effective. Do you lead with ideas you wish to execute and let others lead with theirs? Are you willing to take chances and let other people take them too?

2. Encourage a common goal

According to Kouzes and Posner's research, concepts that pique people's curiosity are more likely to motivate them than threats or rewards. It's not so much about having a vision as it is about successfully conveying it to others. Prominent leaders focus on the future and aim to instill passion, enthusiasm, and emotion in others. They strive to enlist others in this feeling of common purpose.

They are going to:

Describe an uplifting and ennobling future in which people are inspired by the organization's or team's vision.
Draw support for this shared vision from others by appealing to their beliefs, passions, aspirations, and values.
It is simple to focus too much on creating the ideal language for a vision and objective and not enough time on actually communicating it. Could you restate the mission of your organization? To what extent do you attempt to spread it to others?

3. Permit others to take action
Leaders use others to accomplish their goals rather than trying to do it all themselves. However, they don't only accomplish this by reciting the vision statement; inspiration

and admonition are insufficient. People need to be encouraged to act on their ideas and made to feel capable of doing so. Success requires teamwork and relationship-based work.

Being a leader will require you to:

Encourage cooperation by encouraging cooperative objectives and fostering trust within and between teams as well as between leaders and members.
Empower others by giving them access to knowledge and resources, as well as by making them more visible and discreet.
Who on your team or in your organization needs support and motivation to take action? What could propel them into action? Do you have a methodical approach to training individuals and assisting them in gaining competence and confidence?

4. Set an example

Modeling is being willing to lead by example and modeling the behaviors you want other people to follow before requesting that they do so. Individuals are more likely to believe what their leaders routinely demonstrate than what they hear them say. Prominent leaders ought to exhibit the intended methodology, with particular emphasis on:

Be a role model for others by acting in a way that aligns with your organization's and your own values.
Plan for little victories that encourage development in both people and groups, then build on them to keep the momentum going.
Before requesting others to reduce their spending, do you first tighten your own financial belt? If you work in fundraising, do you give to your own cause to set a good example for others to follow?

5. Uplift the soul

Ultimately, Kouzes and Posner proved that when people are enthusiastic about what they are doing, they behave at their best. By sharing their own interests and tales, leaders ignite the ardor of their followers. They take pleasure in commemorating victories of all sizes. They take on challenging tasks while appreciating the efforts of others. They

look for and acknowledge team and individual efforts that have made each project successful.

Regularly recognize and celebrate both team and individual accomplishments, and seek out fun and creative methods to do so.

Consider your most recent staff meeting or newsletter. Did it satisfy this requirement for encouragement? Was it thrilling or just safe and boring? What actions may you do on an organizational level to support the heart?

Finding your strengths and shortcomings in relation to the five leadership practices can help you focus on the few areas that really require improvement. You may go from being an excellent manager to an exceptional leader very fast with awareness, coaching, practice, and feedback.

The five management practices.

It is a well-known fact that managerial aptitude is not a direct correlate with work performance. Many of us have learnt this the hard way—while the majority of us have had terrible bosses at some point, how many of us have had the good fortune to work for a truly inspirational leader who can inspire others and bring out the best in their team? What's more, how can you develop into a leader like that?

Depending on the company culture, the size of the team or organization, the nature of the task or industry, and the specific personalities involved, different management styles will operate in different settings. Still, there are some universals.

Although it's an art, effective management is one that can be learned if you adhere to a few fundamental guidelines. Here are some pointers on improving as a manager that you can implement immediately:

1. Make the appropriate choices
Putting together the greatest team possible is the first step towards making the total more than the sum of its parts. Building a complementing team, assigning the right individuals to the right positions, and coordinating your workforce with the objectives and culture of your company are all important.

"Recruit right," as Westpac project manager Wallace Lee puts it. Verify that each individual matches the culture and, more importantly, possesses the necessary capabilities.

According to Iain Crossing, an organizational consultant with Inspirational Workplaces, understanding how different jobs will contribute to the achievement of your organization's goals will assist set the parameters against which you will interview and evaluate individuals.

One of the biggest factors influencing an organization's capacity to thrive in the face of uncertainty may be the growth of its most important employees. According to Grant Sexton, executive director of Leadership Management Australasia, "a leader's ability to engage people and align the needs of individuals with those of the organization to deliver a united and cohesive front is central to its development."

2. Exhibit compassion

The capacity to listen intently, identify with their emotional state, and communicate your understanding of them is known as empathy. Higher emotional intelligence in managers allows them to establish relationships with team members and foster better trust and transparency.

Being empathetic and transparent should be a major component of your personal brand as a manager. This is the most crucial fundamental ability for managers and leaders, according to Iain Crossing.

Crossing states that "a key determinant in how effective you can be at influencing people, setting them objectives that motivate them, and rewarding them in a way they each actually find motivating" is developing the ability to understand people and connect with them in a genuine, meaningful way.

Actually, a number of research have demonstrated that "emotional competence" is higher among high-performing managers. These tips will help you become a more emotionally intelligent worker.

3. Express yourself clearly

Building connections with your team that are based on honesty, openness, and trust requires effective communication. Crossing states that making time and space for people to chat and ask questions is the first step in effective communication.

Crossing and Lee both stress how crucial it is to lay out your objectives and expectations in detail and to assign roles and duties to individuals in accordance with them. Ultimately, it is impossible to inspire others if they are unaware of your goals. According to Crossing, managers should communicate to staff members what resources and assistance are available to them, establish clear goals that the organization and its members can discuss and negotiate, and clearly tie rewards to performance.

Effective managers must be astute observers to detect how employees are emotionally reacting to a work environment since nonverbal cues are equally as significant as verbal cues. According to Lee, managers must have intuition because employees might not always let you know when they're having difficulties.

There must be open communication between team members as well as between supervisors and their employees. A competent leader listens well and creates an atmosphere where individuals may learn about one another's communication preferences, communication styles, and strengths. Effective managers welcome feedback from their employees and take the time to consider it.

4. Set a good example

According to Iain Crossing, employees will interpret their boss's mood from both verbal and nonverbal cues, thus managers must own up to the environment they foster and influence it with their own actions. This might be as straightforward as how you stand and behave when you first go to work in the morning, or it can be more systematic like defining standards and guidelines for cooperating with one another.

It's also critical to put your beliefs into practice. Your employees cannot be expected to put in more effort than you are willing to. Roll up your sleeves and get your hands dirty once in a while. As Lee states, "You have to earn respect; it doesn't come from your position."

5. Assign

It's critical for managers to understand that they have a limited number of hours in the day and a limited amount of work they can complete alone. Delegating important projects to your team members will save you a ton of time over time, even though you might initially find that doing things alone is faster (especially if your team is new or inexperienced). You will also assist them develop their abilities and realize their full potential by doing this. Delegation does not, however, equate to micromanagement. Wallace Lee cautions against micromanaging as well, saying, "Know when to let your staff run with things - don't interfere."

Allowing your employees to take responsibility for their work and develop unique methods of operation is crucial. Give a clear explanation of the desired result, then let them use their gadgets while periodically checking in to see whether they still need your help. For optimum effect, Crossing suggests, "Delegate responsibility rather than tasks."

Chapter 7

The difference between leadership and management and why they're equally important.

For an organization to achieve strong results, both leadership and management need to be present. With good management and poor leadership the team will lack the motivation to pursue goals. Additionally, without efficient management skills the direction set by a leader risks being unsustainable.

Management is characterized by a focus on the process and the present. Simonet and Tett (2012) describe management as, "providing order and consistency and helping organizations run smoothly; planning and budgeting, organizing and staffing, controlling and problem solving; having a reactive attitude toward problems and goals." This definition suggests that managers are more focused on maintaining function within the organization than providing inspiration or vision for future innovation.

Leadership is characterized by the focus on innovation and the future. In the same article, Simonet and Tett (2012) describe leadership as, "producing change and movement by influencing others to attain goals; establishing direction, and aligning, motivating, and inspiring people; taking an active and visionary stance toward problems and goals; seeking risk and showing empathy toward others." This definition suggests that leaders are more focused on creating change through bold vision, the development of strong interpersonal relationships, building capacity, and inspiring others.

In our community or organization, we may be required to fill the role of manager or leader. Understanding key differences between the two roles is the first step toward the ability to effectively transition between them. The next step is developing and applying strategies to fulfill the responsibilities of each role. This step starts with improving our management and leadership toolkits.

Improving our Managing Toolkit

Andersen et al. (2009) outlined three important components of project managing: planning, organization, and control. Below are some strategies to make sure we address these three key components:

Use group planning and involve as many participants as possible in the design and development process.

Divide the planning process into two stages: the "what" stage and the "how" stage. The "what" stage is the goal planning stage, the determination of what the project's overall goal and objective will be. The "how" stage is the activity planning stage, the creation of the activities that will lead to achieving the project goals.

Identify multiple pathways to achieve the intended goal at the different stages of the project. This will help us adjust future project steps and timely address complications.

Divide large projects into parts and ensure that each activity ties to distinct milestones in the project plan.

Create responsibility descriptions for each team member in the project that outline that person's specific role within the activity and the specific tasks they are responsible for.

Create reporting schedules to keep track of individual and group progress for each activity. Make sure to schedule them at regular intervals so that you do not fall behind.

Improving our Leadership Toolkit

We have adapted some best practices from Coetzer et al. (2017) that may help you improve your leadership capacity.

Be authentic and consistent with your behavior. Do not be afraid to show your true feelings and motivations for the actions you take.

Practice humility. Be modest and aware of your own limitations. Try to act without ego and recognize the skills of your followers.

Show compassion for your followers. Be proactive in praising the work done by others. Take the time to develop personal relationships when possible with your followers and be attentive to challenges and difficulties they may face.

Be altruistic as much as possible. When possible, put the needs of your followers ahead of your own. Look to empower your followers by serving their needs.

Be an active listener. Ask questions to gain perspective and pay attention to both what is said and unsaid by followers. When conducting project meetings, make sure to provide time for followers to reflect on what was said and encourage feedback.

We hope that by using the strategies and best practices presented, you will feel more prepared and confident to serve in either a management or leadership role in your organization's next project.